THE WAITING GAME

Trusting God's Timing

K. Washington

Introduction:

As I sit during my own waiting period, I am struck by the realization that most writers or authors often reflect on their experiences after they have passed through them, expressing lessons learned, and insights gained into their writing. However, I find myself in a unique position- I am experiencing this journey of waiting firsthand, and I feel compelled to share it with others while I am still immersed in it.

Imagine yourself standing on the playground, the vibrant energy of anticipation coursing through your veins as you eagerly await your chance to join the game. Your heart quickens with each selection as the captains are chosen, and the picking begins. With every name called, a surge of hope rises within you, longing for your turn to be next. But as the process unfolds, you find yourself still rooted in place, watching as others are chosen one by one, while you remain unpicked. With each passing moment, a twinge of disappointment pierces your heart, casting a shadow over your eager anticipation. It feels as though time stands still as you witness others moving forward into the game, while you linger on the sidelines, yearning for your moment to shine.

Despite your unwavering dedication-practicing tirelessly, pouring out your heart in fervent prayer, and diligently following the rules-it seems as though you're trapped in a perpetual cycle of waiting.

Each tick of the clock amplifies the blend of longing and frustration that swirls within you, like a tempest raging beneath the surface. Doubt creeps in, whispering insidious questions about the validity of your efforts and the worthiness of your dreams. Yet, amidst the tumult of uncertainty, a flicker of faith remains-a beacon of hope that illuminates the darkness of doubt. You cling to the unwavering belief that God's timing is perfect, even when it feels agonizingly slow.

During this waiting, you grapple with a myriad of emotions-hope mingled with doubt, anticipation tempered by uncertainty. Yet, you refuse to succumb to despair, for deep within your soul, you hold fast to the promise that your waiting is not in vain. You trust in the faithfulness of the One who orchestrates every moment of your life knowing that He holds your future in His hands.

So, with each passing moment, you persevere, fueled by the assurance that your waiting has a purpose beyond your understanding. Though the journey may be fraught with challenges and the destination covered in mystery, you stand firm in the knowledge that God's timing is always worth the wait. As you stand amidst the playground of life, with your eyes fixed on the horizon, you await the moment when His voice will ring out, declaring, "it's YOUR turn."

The decision to write this book didn't come easily. In fact, it emerged from the depths of my own struggle with waiting. Day after day, I grapple with uncertainties, unanswered prayers, and the relentless passage of time. Yet, amidst the tension and frustration, I sense a stirring within me-a desire to not only endure this waiting season but to glean wisdom from it and offer a glimmer of hope to others who may find themselves in similar circumstances.

I am acutely aware of the vunerability that comes with sharing a journey that is still unfolding. There are moments when doubt creeps in, questioning whether I am qualified to speak on a topic that I have yet to fully navigate myself. Yet, during my doubts, there is a quiet assurance-a conviction that this story, raw and unfiltered, has the power to resonate with others who are also waiting for their turn.

So armed with nothing but my own vulnerability and a flicker of faith, I embark on this writing journey. I don't have all the answers, nor do I claim to have mastered the art of waiting. But what I do have is a willingness to be transparent about my struggle, a longing to uncover the lessons buried within the waiting, and a deep-seated belief that there is purpose during uncertainty.

As I pen these words, I am reminded that this book is not just about me-it's about all of us who are navigating the turbulent waters of waiting. Together, we will explore the complexities of patience, the beauty of perseverance, and the profound truth that even during waiting, we are never alone.

And so, with trembling hands and a steadfast resolve, I commit myself to this journey of writing about waiting while I am still in the thick of it. For it is my hope that in sharing my story, I can offer a beacon of light to those who find themselves in the shadows of uncertainty, guiding them towards a deeper understanding of God's faithfulness and the transformative power of waiting.

In a world where instant gratification is the norm, waiting can feel like an inconvenience. But throughout history, people of faith have learned the value of waiting on God's timing. This book explores the concept of waiting on God for your turn, drawing inspiration from stories in the Bible where individuals faced seasons of waiting with patience and trust.

I had been at my job for a few years, and as time went on, I increasingly felt like I didn't belong there. The constant stress started to take a toll on my health, showing up in frequent migraine headaches and high blood pressure. My interactions with coworkers were often fraught with tension, adding to the sense of unease. Deep down, I knew I needed a change.

Amidst this turmoil, I found solace in searching for new job opportunities online. There was one position I had my heart set on for years. Over a span of nineteen years, I had applied for this role so many times, only to receive rejection letters each time. You would think after maybe the first five, I would take it as a sign of it not being the job for me. Yet, something within me refused to give up. This time, I felt a stronger urge to try again. I even confided in a friend about the job, hoping maybe this time things would be different...

The Faith of Abraham

- Story of Abraham and Sarah waiting for the promised son, Isaac, despite their old age (Genesis 15-21)
- Lessons on trusting God's promises even when circumstances seem impossible

The story of Abraham and Sarah waiting for the promised son, Isaac despite their old age is a profound illustration of trusting God's promises in the face of seemingly insurmountable circumstances. In Genesis 15, God promises Abraham that he will have descendants as numerous as the stars in the sky, even though he and Sarah were both advanced in age and childless. This promise is reiterated in Genesis 17 when God changes Abram's name to Abraham, meaning "father of many," and promises that Sarah will bear him a son. However, as years passed without the fulfillment of this promise, doubt began to creep in. Sarah, seeing herself as barren and beyond childbearing age, suggested that Abraham take her servant, Hagar, as a concubine to bear him a child. Abraham complies, and Ishmael is born through Hagar. But Ishmael is not the child of promise, and God reaffirms that Sarah will bear a son and that he will be named Isaac. Despite their wavering faith and attempts to take matters into their own hands, God remains faithful to His promise. When Abraham is 100 years old and Sarah is 90, Isaac is born, fulfilling God's covenant with Abraham.

This story teaches several valuable lessons on trusting God's promises even when circumstances seem impossible:

1. God's timing is perfect: Despite Abraham and Sarah's advanced age and apparent infertility, God's promise was fulfilled exactly as He had planned. This reminds us that God's timing is not bound by human limitations or expectations. He works according to His own perfect timing, which is often different from ours.

2. Faith requires patience: Abraham and Sarah's journey was marked by years of waiting and uncertainty.

Their faith was tested as they waited for God's promise to be fulfilled. Yet, they remained steadfast in their trust in God's faithfulness, even when it seemed unlikely that they would ever have a child.

3. God is faithful, even when we are faithless: Despite Abraham and Sarah's moments of doubt and attempts to fulfill God's promises in their own strength, God remained faithful to His covenant. He fulfilled His promise to them not because of their faithfulness, but because of His own faithfulness and sovereignty.

Our role is to trust and obey. Abraham and Sarah's story highlights the importance of trusting God's promises and obeying His commands, even when they seem impossible or impractical. Their journey of faith serves as a powerful example of what it means to trust in God's goodness and sovereignty, even in the face of uncertainty and doubt.
In essence, the story of Abraham and Sarah waiting for the birth of Isaac is a testament to the power of faith and the faithfulness of God. It challenges us to trust in God's promises even when circumstances seem impossible, knowing that He is faithful to fulfill His word in His perfect timing.

What aspects of your life do you find the most difficult to wait on God, and how might you change your viewpoint by believing in His timing?

Joseph's Journey of Patience

- Joseph's experience of waiting for his dreams to come true, enduring betrayal and imprisionment along the way (Genesis 37-50)
- Insights into maintaining faith and integrity during prolonged waiting periods

Joseph's journey of waiting for his dreams to come true is a profound testament to the challenges and rewards of maintaining faith and integrity during prolonged waiting periods. His story, found in the book of Genesis chapters 37 through 50, offers valuable insights intohow we can navigate seasons of waiting with steadfastness and trust in God's Plan.

The dreamer's vision: Joseph begins his journey as a dreamer, receiving two significant dreams from God that foretell his future greatness. However, his brothers' jealousy leads to betrayal as they sell him into slavery, stripping him of his coat of many colors and casting him into a pit. Despite this betrayal and uncertainty, Joseph holds onto the vision God has given him, believing that one day it will come to fruition.

Enduring trials with integrity: As Joseph is taken to Egypt and sold to Potiphar, an officer of Pharaoh, he faces numerous trials and temptations. Yet, Joseph remains steadfast in his integrity, refusing to compromise his values or betray Potiphar's trust. Even when falsely accused of wrongdoing by Potiphar's wife and thrown into prison, Joesph maintains his integrity and continues to trust in God's plan for his life.

Interpreting dreams in prison: While in prison, Joseph encounters two fellow prisoners, the chief cupbearer and the chief baker, who have dreams that trouble them. Through God's guidance,

Joseph interprets their dreams. accurately, foretelling the restoration of the cupbearer to his position and the execution of the baker. Despite being forgotten by the cupbearer after his release, Joseph remains faithful and continues to trust in God's timing for his own deliverance.

Divine elevation and fulfillment of dreams: Eventually, Joseph's ability to interpret dreams leads him to be summoned before Pharaoh to interpret his troubling dreams.

Forgiveness and reconciliation: Perhaps one of the most powerful aspects of Joseph's story is his ability to forgivehis brothers who had betrayed him. When his brothers come to Egypt looking for food during the famine, Joseph recognizes them but chooses to test their hearts before revealing his identity. Ultimately, Joseph forgives his brothers, acknowledging that what they meant for evil, God used for good, saving many lives. This act of forgiveness and reconciliation demonstrates Joseph's deep faith and trust in God's sovereignty over his life.

Through God's wisdom, Joseph interprets Pharaoh's dreams, predicting seven years of plenty followed by seven years of famine. Impressed by Joseph's wisdom, Pharaoh elevates him to a position of power and authority, second only to Pharaoh himself. In this position, Joseph can fulfill the vision God gave him as a young man, saving Egypt and his own family from starvation during the famine.

In summary, Joseph's experience of waiting for his dreams to come true teaches us valuable lessons about maintaining faith and integrity during extended waiting periods. Through his unwavering trust in God, resilience in the face of adversity, and commitment to righteousness, Joseph demonstrates the power of faith to sustain us through life's trials and ultimately bring about the fulfillment of God's promises in his perfect timing.

How do you stay faithful and optimistic when you're waiting, especially if you don't see results right away?

Moses and the Wilderness

- The Israelites' forty years of wandering in the wilderness before entering the Promised Land (Exodus 13-Deuteronomy 34)
- Discovering the purpose of waiting seasons and finding God's Provision in the midst of uncertainty

The Israelites' forty years of wandering in the wilderness, as recounted in the books of Exodus through Deuteronomy, is a profound narrative rich with lessons about waiting on God and discovering His provision in the middle of uncertainty.

Context waiting: After their their deliverance from slavery in Egypt, the Israelites stood on the brink of entering the Promised Land. However, due to their lack of faith and disobedience, they were condemned to wander in the wilderness for forty years. This period was marked by uncertainty, hardship, and testing.

Purpose of Waiting Seasons

1. Testing and Refinement: The wilderness journey served as a time of testing and refinement for the Israelites. It revealed their true character and exposed areas of unbelief and disobedience. Waiting seasons often serve a similar purpose in our lives, allowing God to refine our faith and character.
2. Dependency on God: In the wilderness, the Israelites were stripped of their self-reliance and forced to depend entirely on God's provision. Waiting seasons remind us of our need for God and teach us to rely on His faithfulness rather than our own strength or resources.
3. Preparation for the Promise: The forty years in the wilderness were not wasted time but a period of preparation for the Promised Land. During this time, God taught the Israelites His laws, established His covenant with them, and prepared them for the challenges they would face in possessing the land. Similarly, waiting seasons in our lives often serve as times of preparation for the blessings God has in store for us.

4. Redirection of Priorities: The wilderness experience forced the Israelites to reevaluate their priorities and allegiance. It was a time for them to turn away from idolatry and renew their commitment to God. Waiting seasons often prompt us to reassess our values and realign our lives with God's purpose.

Gods Provision in Uncertainty

1. Manna from Heaven: Throughout their wilderness journey, God provided daily sustenance for the Israelites in the form of manna, miraculous bread from heaven. This provision demonstrated God's faithfulness to meet their needs even in the most barren and uncertain circumstances.

2. Water from the Rock: When the Israelites were thirsty, God instructed Moses to strike a rock, miraculously providing water for the entire community. This event highlighted God's ability to provide for His people in unexpected and astounding ways, even during scarcity.

3. Divine Guidance: God did not abandon the Israelites in the wilderness but led them with a pillar of cloud by day and a pillar of fire by night. His presence and guidance were constant reminders of His faithfulness and care, even in the face of uncertainty and danger.

In conclusion, the Israelites' forty years of wandering in the wilderness in the wilderness serve as a powerful illustration of the purpose of waiting seasons and the discovery of God's provision amidst uncertainty. Through their story, we learn valuable lessons about faith, dependency on God, preparation, and the assurance that God is with us even in the wilderness moments of life.

How can you wait for God to reveal His purpose or fulfill a promise in your present situation while remaining obedient and patient?

David's Time in the Cave

- David's year of hiding in caves while fleeing from King Saul's pursuit (1 Samuel 18-31)
- Lessons on resilience, faith, and seeking God's guidance during times of waiting and adversity

God's guidance during times of waiting and adversity

Resilience in the face of Adversity: David's journey from being annointed as the future king to fleeing for his life showcases remarkable resilience. Despite facing constant threats to his life and the uncertainty of his future, David remained steadfast in his faith and commitment to God. Instead of succumbing to despair or giving in to fear, he chose to trust in God's faithfulness and provision, even when circumstances seemed dire.

Faith In Uncertainty: Throughout his time in hiding, David's faith in God remained unwavering. Despite the betrayal and opposition, he faced, he clung to the belief that God had a plan and purpose for his life. This unwavering faith sustained him through the uncertainty. David's example challenges us to anchor our faith not in our circumstances but in the unchanging character of God.

Seeking God's Guidance in Every Situation: David's reliance on God's guidance is evident in his actions and decisions during this period. Whether sparing Saul's life when he had the opportunity to kill him or seeking God's direction before taking any major steps, David consistently prioritized seeking God's guidance above all else. His humility and dependence on God's wisdom serve as a powerful reminder of the importance of seeking godly guidance in every aspect of our lives, especially during times of waiting and adversity.

Lesson in patience and trust: David's time in the wilderness taught him invaluable lessons in patience and trust. Instead of rushing ahead or taking matters into his own hands, he learned to wait patiently for God's timing. This waiting period served as a season of refinement, shaping David into the courageous and compassionate leader he would later become.

His journey underscores the truth that God's timing is always perfect, and His plans far exceed our own understanding.

David's experience of hiding in caves while fleeing from King Saul's pursuit, as depicted in the books of 1 Samuel 18-31, provides profound insights into resilience, faith, and seeking God's guidance amidst adversity. His example inspires us to remain steadfast in our faith, trust in God's promises, and seek His guidance even in the most challenging seasons of life.

How do you trust God's timing and embrace the "cave seasons" of your life when tomorrow looks uncertain?

The Promised Fulfilled

Elisabeth & Zechariah

- The miraculous birth of John the Baptist to elderly parents, Elisabeth and Zechariah (Luke 1)
- Encouragement to remain faithful and expectant even when waiting seems prolonged

The miraculous birth of John the Baptist to elderly parents, Elisabeth and Zechariah, as recorded in Luke 1, provides a profound example of remaining faithful and expectant during prolonged waiting.

Elisabeth and Zechariah were both righteous and devout individuals who followed God's commandments faithfully. Despite their dedication to God, they faced a deeply personal trial: infertility. In the culture of their time, infertility was not only emotionally challenging but also carried a sense of shame and societal stigma. Despite their prayers for a child, they remained childless, and as they grew older, the hope of having a child seemed increasingly impossible. However, their story takes a miraculous turn when Zechariah, serving as a priest in the temple, is visited by the angel Gabriel. The angel announces to Zechariah that his prayers have been heard and that Elisabeth will conceive and bear a son, whom they are to name John. This news comes as a shock to Zechariah, who questions the angel's message due to his disbelief in the possibility of a child at their advanced age. As a result of his doubt, Zechariah is temporarily struck mute until the prophecy is fulfilled.

Even though they don't believe, Elisabeth and Zechariah hold onto the promise given by the angel. Elisabeth conceives, and in her old age, she bears him a son, just as Gabriel had foretold. This miraculous birth not only brings joy to Elisabeth and Zechariah but also serves as a sign of God's faithfulness and power to fulfill His promises.

The story of Elisabeth and Zechariah encourages us to remain faithful and expectant in our own waiting seasons, even when circumstances seem impossible of prolonged. Here are some key insights drawn from their story:

God's Timing is Perfect: In spite of the long years of waiting, God's timing was impeccable. He chose to fulfill His promise at a time when it seemed least likely, highlighting His sovereignty over time and circumstances.

God Keeps His Promises: The fulfillment of Gabriel's prophecy demonstrated God's faithfulness to His word. Elisabeth and Zechariah's story reminds us that God's promises are trustworthy and will come to pass in His perfect timing.

Faithfulness In Waiting: Elisabeth and Zechariah remained faithful to God even during disappointment and uncertainty. Their unwavering prayer and dedication to God in the face of adversity is a great model for us to follow when we are waiting on God.

Miracles Still Happen: The miraculous birth of John the Baptist reminds us that God is still in the business of performing miracles. Even when situations seem hopeless, God can intervene and bring about extraordinary outcomes beyond our expectations.

In conclusion, Elisabeth and Zechariah's story inspires us to not give up hope and faith, believing that God is still at work while we wait. We should continue to be obedient, hopeful, and trusting in God's perfect timing as we wait for His promises to be revealed in our lives.

Where in your life do you find it difficult to trust God's timing, and how can you rely on patience and faith as you wait?

Jesus' Ministry of Preparation

- Jesus' years of preparation before beginning his public ministry (Luke 2:41-52)
- Understanding the importance of spiritual growth and readiness during seasons of waiting

Jesus' years of preparation before beginning his public ministry, as depicted in Luke 2:41-52, provide a profound insight into the significance of spiritual growth and readiness during seasons of waiting. The passage, often referred to as the "Finding in the Temple," offers a glimpse into Jesus' early life and the events leading up to his ministry.

Context of the Passage: At the age of twelve, Jesus accompanies his parents to Jerusalem for the Passover festival. After the festival ends, Mary and Joseph, assuming Jesus is with their relatives or fellow travelers, begin their journey home. It's not until they realize Jesus is missing that they return to Jerusalem to look for him. After three days, they find Jesus in the temple, engaging in deep discussions with the teachers.

Spiritual Growth and Understanding: Despite his young age, Jesus demonstrates remarkable wisdom and understanding of Scripture. He engages the teachers in dialogue, asking questions and offering insights that astound those around him. This incident highlights Jesus' deep spiritual connection and his early awareness of his divine identity and mission.

Preparation for Ministry: Jesus' time in the temple foreshadows his future ministry. It shows his deep commitment to God and his desire to learn and teach about spiritual matters. These formative years were crucial in shaping Jesus' understanding of his purpose and preparing him for the challenges he would face in his ministry.

The Importance of Waiting and Preparation: Jesus' early years were not marked by public acclaim or visible ministry. Instead, they were characterized by quiet preparation and growth. This underscores the importance of atience and readiness during seasons of waiting. Like Jesus, we are called to cultivate our relationship with God, deepen our understanding of His word, and grow in spiritual maturity, even when our calling or purpose may not yet be fully realized.

Application to Our Lives: Just as Jesus spent years preparing for his ministry, we too are called to embrace seasons of waiting as opportunities for spiritual growth and preparation. These times of waiting may seem uneventful or even frustrating, but they are essential for shaping us into the people God intends for us to be. By remaining faithful, seeking God diligently, and allowing Him to work in our lives, we can be confident that He is preparing us for the plans and purposes He has for us.

In summary, Jesus' early years of preparation before his public ministry teaches us the importance of spiritual growth and readiness during seasons of waiting. Through his example, we are encouraged to embrace these times as opportunities for deepening our relationship with God and preparing ourselves for the fulfillment of His purposes in our lives.

How can you embrace waiting seasons as moments to grow in our relationship with God and get ready for His purposes instead of rushing through them alone?

Paul's Patient Endurance

- Paul's perseverance through trials, imprisonment, and waiting for God's timing in ministry (2 Corinthians 11:23-33, Acts 28)
- Insights into finding purpose and strength in waiting through faith and perseverance

Paul's life serves as a powerful example perseverance through trials, imprisonment, and waiting for God's timing in ministry. In 2 Corinthians 11:23-33, Paul recounts the numerous hardships he endured for the sake of spreading the Gospel. He faced beatings, imprisonments, shipwrecks, hunger, and danger from various sources. Despite these challenges, Paul remained steadfast in his faith and commitment to his calling. One key aspect of Paul's perseverance was his unwavering belief in the purpose behind his suffering. He understood that his trials were not meaningless but were part of God's plan for his life and ministry. This perspective gave him strength and endurance to press on, even in the face of seemingly insurmountable obstacles.

Paul's imprisonment, particularly his time in Rome as recorded in Acts 28, is a striking example of waiting for God's timing. While under house arrest, Paul continued to preach the Gospel to those who visited him, demonstrating his unwavering commitment to his calling despite being confined. He used this time to write letters to churches and individuals, including his powerful letter to the Philippians, which is filled with themes of joy, perseverance, and contentment in all circumstances.

Through Paul's example, we gain insights into finding purpose and strength in waiting through faith and resilience:

Trust in God's Sovereignty: Paul trusted in God's sovereignty over his life and ministry, believing that God was in control even during adversity. this trust enabled him to endure trials with patience and hope, knowing that God's purposes would ultimately prevail.

Focus on the Eternal: Paul's perspective was shaped by an eternal mindset. He understood that the sufferings of this present life were temporary compared to the eternal glory that awaited believers. This perspective gave him the strength to persevere through hardships, knowing that they were producing an eternal weight of glory (2 Corinthians 4:17).

Prayer and Dependence on God: Throughout his trials, Paul maintained a deep connection with God through prayer. He relied on God's strength to sustain him and found comfort in knowing that God was with him in every circumstance. This dependence on God fueled his perserverence and enabled him to endure even in the darkest moments.

Focus on the Mission: Despite his pesonal hardships, Paul remained focused on his mission to spread the Gospel and build up the body of Christ. He saw his suffering as an opportunity to advance the kingdom of God and bring glory to Christ. This sense of purpose gave him the motivation to persevere even when facing intense opposition.

In conclusion, Paul's life exemplifies the power of faith and perseverance in the midst of trials and waiting. By following his example and trusting in God's sovereignty, focusing on the eternal, maintaining a deep connection with God through prayer, and remaining committed to the mission, we can find purpose and strength in waiting for God's timing in our own lives.

While you wait for God to fulfill a promise or give you insight in a certain area of your life, how can you continue to be obedient and productive?

...Months have passed with no word from the company, and I continued to endure the stress of my current job. The physical symptoms persisted, but I clung to my faith, believing that God had a plan for me. I was convinced that this time, things would work out in my favor. Then, in a twist of fate, the friend I told about the job received an offer letter from the company I had been pursuing for years. It stung a little, but I held onto my faith, telling myself that my time was coming. I continued to talk to God, trusting that He would guide me to where I needed to be.

A few more months went by, and then it finally happened. I received an offer for the position I had been waiting on for nineteen years. The joy and relief I felt were indescribable. Reflecting on the journey, I realized the significance of trusting in God's timing. Had the opportunity come to me nineteen years ago, I might not have been in the right season to embrace or sustain it. Like Joseph, who needed years of trials to prepare for his leadership, or Moses, who spent 40 years in the wilderness before leading the Israelites, my time of waiting allowed me to mature, gain perspective, and become the person capable of handling the opportunity when it finally arrived. I've come to understand that sometimes God's delays are His way of ensuring I'm equipped to steward His blessings wisely, avoiding mistakes that could cost me.

Waiting on God for your turn is not passive idleness but an active journey of trust, growth, and preparation. By studying the stories of those who waited faithfully in the Bible, we can learn to embrace our own seasons of waiting with hope and confidence in God's perfect timing. As we wait, let us remember the words of Isaiah 40:31, "But they who wait for the Lord shall renew their strength; they shall mount up with wings like eagles; they shall run and not be weary; they shall walk and not faint."

These words remind us that as we wait on God, He strengthens us, enabling us to soar above our circumstances, run with perseverance, and walk with unwavering faith.

Each story, whether it's Abraham and Sarah's patient anticipation for the promised son, Joseph's endurance through trials, or Paul's perseverance in ministry despite imprisonment, teaches us something profound about waiting on God. It's not just about the result; it's about the transformation that occurs within us as we wait.

So, let's embrace our waiting seasons with courage and dedication, knowing that God is with us every step of the way, shaping us into who He has called us to be.

Be blessed,

K Washington

Made in United States
North Haven, CT
11 December 2024

61370582R00022